ENDURING LIFE OR ENJOYING LIFE?

*How to never be down, discouraged, or depressed
another day in your life!*

JIM FREASE

Unless otherwise indicated, all Scripture quotations are taken from the *King James Version* of the Bible.

PO Box 247
Mount Juliet, TN 37121
www.joychurch.net

Printed in the United States of America

Frease, Jim.
Enduring Life or Enjoying Life?: How to never be down, discouraged, or depressed another day in your life! / Jim Frease.
p. 108
ISBN 978-0-9983918-1-6
1. Motivational 2. Inspirational. 3. Christian Living.
First Edition
First Printing 2017

CONTENTS

FOREWORD

I have known Jim Frease for more than a quarter of a century, and I can honestly say he is the most joy-filled pastor I have ever met in my ministry. And as the years have passed, it has seemed that Jim's joy just keeps increasing.

As I read the book *Enduring Life or Enjoying Life?*, I kept thinking, if anyone has a right to author a book on this subject, it is Jim Frease! Not only has this joy affected Jim and his wife Anne, but that same joy can also be sensed throughout the church he pastors—which is aptly named Joy Church.

The subtitle of Jim's book—*How To Never Be Down, Discouraged, or Depressed Another Day of Your Life!*—is also aptly named because Jim lived it before he ever wrote about it. After fighting depression in his own life, Jim came to a moment when he decided he would not live that way anymore. That decision more than two decades ago permanently ended depression in his life and set him on a supernatural journey of joy.

And I can tell you from personal experience that the joy working in Jim's life is infectious! His audio teachings have been played many hours in my home. When I simply hear him speak, it brings an impartation of joy into my life. It is truly supernatural, and this great deposit of exuberant joy that Jim possesses can be released in your life as well!

In this book, Jim shows you how to have joy and how to sustain that joy every day for the rest of your life. I have read every page of this book, and I found it both personally challenging and directional as Jim shows the way to a life that is above average and consistently full of joy.

My life is richer because of the joyful influence of Jim Frease, and I'm honored that he has asked me to write the foreword to his book. I believe that anyone who reads what he has to say about his favorite subject will be the better for it. His effect on me personally has been so profound that when I hear anyone speak of joy, I immediately think of Jim Frease. I am confident that this book will have the same life-giving effect on others that it has had on me.

Rick Renner
Author and Pastor
Moscow Good News Church
Moscow, Russia

To my precious wife, Anne, who has enjoyed the journey
with me for almost three decades.

To my only son, Johnathan,
who has been such a joy in my life.

INTRODUCTION

Enduring Life or Enjoying Life?

I have lost my way to depression. I suppose if I looked hard enough, I could find that depressing road again. However, I have thrown away the map. As of the writing of this book, it's been 22 years since I have been discouraged or depressed! As soon as I make that statement, it normally garners very visceral responses from those who hear it:

Response #1: *"He has a gift"* or *"He is by nature a very happy person"*.

My reply: I do have a gift, but it's something you have, too! You clearly did not know me before I knew Jesus. I was a depressed alcoholic. Even as a young believer, I would have frequent bouts of being *very* bummed out.

Response #2: *"I get depressed just hearing that you haven't been depressed for 22 years!"* or *"I was depressed just yesterday. I must be sub-spiritual, inadequate, or unworthy."*

My reply: God is no respecter of persons (see Acts 10:4). He wants to do for you what He has done for me. You are not unworthy! Just don't try to receive from God based on what you have or have not done. Always receive from God based on what He has done for you.

Response #3: *"I'll have what he's drinking!"*

That is the purpose of this book: to tell you how to walk this joyful journey out for yourself. If you have a good heart and I tell you *what* to do without telling you *how* to do it, you'll be very *frustrated*. However, if I tell you what to do **and** how to do it, you'll be very *motivated*. This book is dedicated to you and your marvelous journey of going from *enduring* to *enjoying* your life!

CHAPTER 1

My Journey to Joy

Many years ago, I was in the Mexico City airport with my beautiful wife Anne, traveling to a conference to speak. I was lugging three large suitcases to check in for our flight. We got in a very long line and finally made it to the check-in counter only to find out we were in the wrong line. Frustrated but determined, we lumbered our way to the next long line, burdened by the increasingly heavy suitcases I was carrying (this was before the days of wheels on luggage).

Finally, we made our way to the front of the second line, only to find that, once again, we were in the wrong line! That's when I felt the first significant pain in my heart: angina accompanied by irregular heartbeats and shortness of breath. I stopped, prayed, and asked Anne to agree with me in prayer. I certainly did not want to go to a hospital in the middle of Mexico City! Cautiously, we boarded our small airplane and headed to a little city called San Luis Potosi, Mexico. In the middle of the flight, a second wave of severe heart symptoms hit me: much more intense pain shooting down my left arm and irregular heartbeats accompanied by greater shortness of breath.

Besides me and Anne, there were only six others on this flight: two pilots, two flight attendants, and two businessmen—all of whom spoke only Spanish. We were literally in the middle of nowhere; we couldn't go

> *Put the Word of God in you when you don't need it so that it comes out when you do!*

to a hospital even if we wanted to! In the midst of these very alarming symptoms, I simply began to speak the promises of God concerning healing: "by His stripes we were healed" (1 Peter 2:24). You don't know when the storms of life will come your way (see Matthew 7:24–27). Put the Word of God in you when you don't need it so that it comes out when you do!

God got us through this tumultuous flight, and I was able to preach at the conference. However, the situation only spiraled down from there. I knew what the Bible teaches on divine healing and had taught a class on healing at World Changers Bible Institute. I had prayed for thousands of people and watched God physically heal them. I had even had the privilege of praying for two blind people, upon which God miraculously restored their sight. I was convinced that God is not a car-wrecking, cancer-causing Creator, but a loving, life-giving Lord (see Acts 10:38). Even so, I could relate to the little woman with the issue of blood, where the Bible tells us she didn't get better but rather grew worse (see Mark 5:26).

This was such a difficult, discouraging, and depressing time in my life. I have always been athletic and involved in weight training since I was 15 years old. I love to get outside and have fun. But, for the first time in my life, I physically could not. I became very emaciated, and I could barely walk and barely talk. On rare occasions, I would try to get out of our small apartment and walk at the mall with my wife. I couldn't go 400 feet without experiencing angina and irregular heartbeats.

I have been in ministry for 31 years and have always loved to teach the Bible, but during that horrible period, my voice was relegated to barely above a whisper. I would have to sit down with a pillow wedged under my left arm to help the circulation.

My precious wife had to do all of the household chores during that time, and she had to give me nightly massages to enhance blood flow (after I was healed, I didn't tell her for six more months just so I could keep getting massages). We were believing God daily, continuing to study and speak the Scripture on healing, yet for six long months, I didn't get better but progressively worse!

I remember towards the end of that darkest part of my life, I became very depressed. However, I knew the joy of the Lord was my strength (see Nehemiah 8:10). If I was going to beat this thing, I was going to need the strength to continue (see Hebrews 6:12, 10:35).

I am now in my mid-fifties, and my health is completely restored. I jog between three and four hours every week and weight train four times every week. My energy is through the roof, and I can do things I couldn't do when I was in my twenties! Through the darkest hours of my life, God imparted to me wisdom from the Word that saved my life.

As we journey through the remainder of this book, I endeavor to impart this to you, reader: you can also lose your way to depression and find your way to enjoying the rest of your life!

CHAPTER 2

Joy: What Is It?

Understanding God's muscle for life's heavy lifting

We are honored to have many police officers attend our church. Many of them are S.W.A.T. officers. The S.W.A.T. unit, Special Weapons and Tactics, is an elite group of officers who continually challenge themselves with rigorous physical training. These officers know that their favorite pastor (me) is very much devoted to physically challenging himself as well. Occasionally, they will come to me with their latest arduous training regimen to challenge me and see how I fare.

One of their latest training tools is employed by the Navy SEALs, so you know it's tough! This rigorous training requires 50 strict (nose to the ground) push-ups, 50 strict sit-ups, 15 pull-ups, 25 dips, 160 butterfly kicks, and military pressing a 45-pound metal plate over your head 40 times.

You must do this routine start to finish without stopping. Their record time for accomplishing this was three minutes and 59 seconds. The challenge was on. On my first attempt, I recorded a time of four minutes and one second—so close! With my competitive attitude, I had to do it again. This time I tied the record at three minutes and 59 seconds! Not bad for a pastor well into his fifties!

> *Joy is the muscle of God designed to do life's heavy lifting.*

My son has just entered his teenage years, and I am passing on my passion for exercise and weight training to him. He is already developing some muscles, but when it comes to the real heavy lifting, Dad still has to step in and take over. In much the same way, joy is the muscle of God designed to do life's heavy lifting.

The Greek word for "joy" is *chara*. It implies an inward delight or party. The Bible tells us in Nehemiah 8:10, "...the *joy of the Lord* is your strength." This is not simply human joy. This is the joy of the Lord, His special muscle designed to give you strength! Do you remember the old Christian song? "This joy that I have, the world didn't give it to me...the world didn't give it, the world can't take it away!" These lyrics of that song are true: this is the Lord's joy, His muscle designed to give you strength for everyday living and in adverse circumstances.

The Word of God tells us, "Rejoice in the Lord always and again I say rejoice" (Philippians 4:4). Notice from this powerful verse where our joy should be placed: in the *Lord*, not in our *circumstances*. The reason I have not been discouraged or depressed for well over two decades is because of where I place my joy.

> *Circumstances come and circumstances go. Circumstances are up and circumstances are down.*
>
> *But the Lord never changes!*

My joy is in Someone who *never* changes: the Lord! Circumstances come and circumstances go. Circumstances are up and circumstances are down. But the Lord *never* changes!

If the Lord never changes, and my joy is placed in the Lord, why should my joy ever change?

Think about the last time you were in a bad mood (for some of you, this may be a quick memory). I am going to say something that may just put you in a bad mood. The last time you were in a bad mood was because you were thinking about *yourself*. You might say, "No, I was thinking about my mean spouse!" No, you were thinking about how your mean spouse made you feel. "I was thinking about my mean boss." No, you were thinking about how your mean boss made you feel. "I was thinking about the horrible circumstances I am presently facing." No, you were thinking about how those horrible circumstances made you feel.

Your joy has been placed in the wrong thing. Your spouse, your boss, and your circumstances can be up, down, and all around, but the Lord never changes (see Hebrews 13:8). Rejoice *in the Lord!*

> *The last time you were in a bad mood was because you were thinking about yourself.*

Please don't mistake me, I don't want you to mix up joy and happiness, two very different concepts. The culture will tell you they are one and the same, but biblically speaking, they are quite different. You should always be joyful, but there are times you shouldn't be happy.

Let me illustrate.

Let's say you are at your mother-in-law's funeral. Despite her death, you should still be joyful. If you are happy, on the other hand, people might think you had something to do with it! If you are dancing a little jig while singing a line from The Wizard of Oz, "Ding dong, the witch is dead," you may be going away for a long time, too.

Think of the word "happiness." The root of this word is "happenings." Sometimes, our happenings are wonderful. It's easy to be happy when all of your bills are paid, the family is healthy, you are on vacation, and your favorite college football team just won the national championship!

It's an entirely different thing when your circumstances are less than stellar.

A few years ago, I was working late at the church. When I finally returned home, I was eager to get inside and see my wonderful family. It was dark, I was in a hurry, and I accidentally slammed the car door on my finger. It was stuck! I couldn't get to my keys, it was very late, and I was too embarrassed to cry out for help. I actually had to use my foot to push off the car which gave me enough force to dislodge my finger. I can promise you I was not happy, but I truthfully maintained my joy. My dignity? That's an entirely different matter!

Over the last 25 years, I have been bitten by a shark, chased by an alligator, gone through a miscarriage with my wife, experienced heavy betrayal by those to whom I have given my life, and faced my father's going home to be with Jesus.

> *You should always be joyful, but there are times you shouldn't be happy.*

I certainly was not happy about any of those incidents (it was especially no fun to be bitten by the shark—while he was relatively small, his teeth were relatively sharp!), but through all of them, I chose joy.

CHAPTER 3

You Have It!

Quit trying to get what you already got!

I am an avid fisherman. One sunny afternoon on my day off, I was with my family out on our boat. I was fishing, Anne was reading a book, and my son, Johnathan, was swimming around the boat. At that time, John was about seven years old. I had taught him to swim, but since we were in a lake, he had his lifejacket firmly secured around him.

I had just caught a fish and was very focused on bringing the fish into the boat, and my wife was engrossed in her book when we suddenly looked up and could not see our son anywhere! If you are a parent and you've ever briefly lost sight of your child in a crowded mall, you know the force of fear that tries to immediately grip your soul! We cried out, "John, where are you?!"

From my experience as a lifeguard, I was fully cognizant of the inherent dangers of a swimmer drowning in a lake. In a pool, you can clearly see a submerged body, but in a lake, if your eyes are not directly on that swimmer when he goes under, your chances of rescuing him are next to zero. My wife and I cried out our son's name louder and louder, but still we could not locate him anywhere! Over and over we called for John, and just as I was about to dive into the deep lake and look for his body, we heard a timid, little voice call back, "Mommy, Daddy, here I am!"

As a loving parent, that was the best sentence I had heard in a long time! You see, John had been hiding under the front bow of our boat, playing a little game with his mom and dad. I immediately grabbed him by his arm and hoisted him into the boat, filled with mixed emotions. I was overjoyed because he was safe, but I was going to ground him until he was 42 years old! Our precious son was there the entire time. I was searching for something I *already had*.

The Bible tells us in Galatians 5:22–23, "But the fruit of the Spirit is love, joy, peace, longsuffering, gentleness, goodness, faith, meekness, temperance: against such there is no law." When you were born again, Jesus supernaturally placed His fruit on the inside of your spirit. That's His joy that He placed on the inside of you—quit trying to get what you already got! It may be poor English, but it's good Bible!

This has been one of the devil's biggest tactics ever since the Garden of Eden. Do you remember when the devil tempted Eve? He told Eve that if she partook of the fruit,

"...ye shall be as gods" (Genesis 3:5). Herein lies the trickery of the devil. They *already were like God!* The Bible tells us that they were created in the *image* and *likeness* of God (see Genesis 1:26). So the enemy was trying to deceive them into getting something *they already had.*

> *Quit trying to get what you already got!*

Very little has changed. The devil still does this today. You become down, dismayed, or depressed, and he tries to convince you that you need more joy. Your enemy tries to put you in the position of waiting on God for more joy. So here you sit, waiting on God, while God is sitting in Heaven waiting on you to release what you already have!

The Bible tells us in Philemon verse 6, "That the communication of thy faith may become effectual by the acknowledging of every good thing which is in you in Christ Jesus." In other words, my faith is enhanced when I acknowledge that God has already placed His joy inside my heart. Our Heavenly Father is waiting on us to acknowledge it and release it!

A number of years ago, I was in Missouri, ministering at a church. I was outdoors, praying before the service, and God clearly spoke to my heart concerning revival, "My people are waiting on something *coming down from above.* I am waiting on something *flowing out from within.*"

Think about it for a moment. He has given us His:

- Power (Acts 1:8)

- Armor (Ephesians 6:11)

- Spirit (1 Corinthians 6:19–20)

- Word (2 Timothy 3:16)

- Anointing (1 John 2:20)

- Righteousness (2 Corinthians 5:21)

- Love (Romans 5:5)

- Peace (Philippians 4:6–7)

- Fruit (Galatians 5:22–23)

- Joy!

The Bible says, "...that my joy might *remain* in you..." (John 15:11).

Quit trying to get what you already got!

> *"My people are waiting on something coming down from above. I am waiting on something flowing out from within."*

CHAPTER 4

Choose It!

It's a choice to rejoice!

A few years ago, we were driving to Oklahoma to participate in a ministry conference. As we were traveling from Tennessee to Oklahoma, an unexpected March ice storm arose. For safety purposes, we stayed overnight in a hotel in Memphis and then consulted with the Arkansas Highway Patrol to see if it was clear to continue to Oklahoma. The Highway Patrol gave us the green light to travel, indicating only that travel would simply be a bit slower. We soon found out just how slow it would become!

As we crossed the Tennessee border into Arkansas, we noticed that traffic had completely stopped. As we approached the stopped vehicles we noticed that about six inches of ice had built up on the highway, which almost turned it into a skating rink! Traffic had come to a complete stop. Little by little, our delay turned into hours. As our delay grew longer, I decided to redeem the time and get some ministerial work done. I made frequent calls to my Executive Pastor with various ministry assignments.

As I called, I would regularly give him an update on our travels (or the lack thereof). As the hours went by, he noticed a consistency in my voice and interaction. He told me that I sounded consistently joyful as the hours plodded slowly by. All told, we moved a grand total of about 30 miles in *14 hours*! Invariably, whenever I tell this story, people will ask me, "What did you and your family do about going to the bathroom over that 14-hour period?" To which I reply, "What happened on I-40 *stays* on I-40."

You see, throughout the cold and boring 14-hour marathon, the reason I could consistently maintain my joy was because I *chose* to! The Bible tells us, "This is the day the Lord has made, I *will* rejoice and be glad in it" (Psalm 118:24). In everyday language, it is a *choice to rejoice*!

> ## *It is a choice to rejoice!*

Before you dismiss this as some flippant little verse, let me give you some background on the verse so you can see its true power. Immediately preceding Jesus' crucifixion, He celebrated Passover with His disciples. Afterward, the Bible tells us that He and His disciples sang a hymn (see Matthew 26:30). While I certainly can't tell you the melody of this hymn, I can tell you the lyrics. "Pastor Jim, you don't look a day over 40 (you might want to check your glasses), how can you possibly know what lyrics they sang?!" It was a Jewish custom to sing Psalm 113 through Psalm 118 after partaking of Passover. Almost at the very end of Psalm 118, you find in verse 24, "This is the day the Lord hath made, I will rejoice and be glad in it." The day that David the psalmist was speaking of was the day Jesus was to be crucified.

Jesus knew the Old Covenant Scriptures very well, so He knew the excruciating event about to befall Him. He knew Isaiah 50:6 and Psalm 22, detailing a scourging so torturous that His very beard would be ripped from His face, and large chunks of skin would be ripped from His body to the point where he could see his exposed ribs. In the days of Jesus (see Matthew 26, 1 Peter 2:24), one would use a whip with nine tails—each tail tipped with a piece of sharp bone or rock—and thrash the tails around the victim's body. When the whip was extracted, it would tear away hunks of flesh from the person being scourged.

Jesus knew Isaiah 52:14, where the Scripture told Him that He would be so viciously beaten that He would be unrecognizable to those who gazed upon Him. However, Jesus also knew Nehemiah 8:10, which tells us, "The joy of the Lord is your strength." As our Jesus sang Psalm 118:24, it had a special and powerful meaning to Him, and it was part of what sustained Him through the worst suffering anyone has ever had to endure. If the power of that Scripture could get Jesus through the most excruciating (the origin of the word "excruciating" comes from the word "cross") day in the annals of mankind, it can get you through whatever you are facing!

Notice, "This is the day." It is absolutely vital that we choose joy on a *daily* basis!

Have you ever seen one of those old western movies in which the hero would have a gunfight with the villain at sunset? With the sun slowly setting, the hero would face his adversary with a squint in his eye. "Go ahead; make my day!" he would say. Then, whoever drew their pistol first would obviously win that battle.

Such is the joy-filled life. If you want to win the battle against your adversary, you must *draw first*! There are days when it seems like the devil and all his hordes are sitting at the foot of your bed just waiting for you to wake up so they can remind you of all the depressing things you are presently facing in life: the bills, the kids, the economy, the doctor's report... on and on, the incessant chides of your enemy ring in your ears!

> *If you want to win the battle against your adversary, you must draw first!*

If you are not cautious, you will allow the devil to set the course of your day for you. Draw first!

Don't let the devil determine your day...
draw first!

Don't let negative circumstances determine your day...
draw first!

Don't let your mother-in-law determine your day...
draw first!

Don't let your own feelings determine your day...
draw first!

Never feel your way into acting; *act* your way into *feeling*! Get up and declare before your adversary, before your negative circumstances, before your feelings, and even before your mother-in-law: this is the day the Lord has made. I *will* rejoice and be glad in it! After all, it is a *choice* to *rejoice*!

CHAPTER 5

Count It!

*Give God thanks not because
of what happened to you,
but in spite of what happened to you.*

I am an older dad. My son John was born when I was forty years old (as a matter of fact, I just recently convinced my son that I am not his grandpa!). Because of our adventures in faith, in following the plan of God for our lives, Anne and I waited for many years to have our first child. After many years and significant pressure from wannabe grandparents, we decided it was time to have a baby. Shortly thereafter, Anne became pregnant! After a few days, we went to our obstetrician to have an ultrasound, and Anne's pregnancy was confirmed.

It was Christmastime, so we scheduled a trip to Tulsa to see Anne's parents and surprise them with a picture of their new grandchild. We carefully wrapped the little ultrasound picture in festive wrapping, excited to share the wonderful news. Anne's parents opened the package, and to their delight, discovered that they were going to be grandparents. Everyone hugged and some cried. One day later, on Christmas Eve, Anne began to bleed and the baby was miscarried. We now had the very unpleasant task of informing our family while dealing with this tragic situation. One by one, we shared the bad news with family members, and one by one, we cheered *them* up. We traveled home to Tennessee and visited our doctor, who confirmed the sad news. We then proceeded to cheer him up as well. Anne and I knew we needed to give thanks to the Lord—not *because* of what had happened, but *in spite* of what had happened.

Now, I knew this was not God's best for us (see Exodus 23:25–26, Deuteronomy 7:13, 28:4,11, Psalm 113:9, 128:3, 139:13), so I began to ask God what spiritual "holes" we needed to "sew up" in order to hold a healthy baby full term. The Lord clearly revealed to me a couple of spiritual "tweaks" we needed to make. Shortly thereafter, Anne and I began the process of conceiving again, and within two weeks, Anne was once again pregnant! This time, the pregnancy was truly supernatural. Anne had no morning sickness, and her pregnancy was very easy!

Nearing the due date, Anne and I were holding our monthly prayer meeting at World Changers Bible Institute, and she began to have light contractions. Nothing too significant, so we went home and settled in for the evening.

The contractions began to come a little more frequently and with greater intensity. It was nearing midnight, and I uttered a "man comment" I have yet to live down. Those of you reading this book who have ever had a baby, brace yourselves; you're going to want to slap me! I said to Anne ever so gently, "Why don't we just go to sleep and then head off to the hospital in the morning?"

Please forgive me, ladies, I am simply a man who doesn't happen to be the brightest crayon in the box!

Anne vehemently replied, "I think we need to go now!" (Some people are so self-consumed).

We quickly traveled to the hospital. They admitted Anne and immediately took her to the triage where they discovered she was just four centimeters dilated. Normally, a pregnant woman needs to be about 10 centimeters dilated before giving birth, and the average time it takes to dilate is about one centimeter per hour. Therefore, I figured in all my brilliant manhood that it would be a good six hours before Anne gave birth.

Ladies, brace yourselves for "mantastic" event number two!

I went down to park our car, and because I knew we were going to be there for a while, I took my sweet time finding a good parking space (I know, I am a man. Did I mention I may not be the sharpest knife in the drawer?).

I finally made it up to Anne's hospital room at 1:50 a.m. As soon as I walked into her room, Anne's water instantly broke. Four pushes and just ten minutes later, at 2:00 a.m., Anne gave birth to our son Johnathan.

It happened so quickly that Anne looked at me and asked where we were in the birthing process. I looked at her and gently told my wife that our boy had already arrived. She literally had no idea that she had just given birth. John's birth occurred so fast that our doctor did not even have time to arrive; it was just me (barely) and two nurses. I'll never forget that when John came out of his mother's womb, one of the nurses asked if I wanted to cut the umbilical cord, to which I politely declined. She was very adamant and told me that I would regret it if I didn't cut the cord. Fourteen years later, I can honestly tell you that I regret that I *did* cut the cord. To this day, I still have nightmares about it!

Anne did not need an epidural (I asked if I could have hers), and, because she had no pain, did not even need Tylenol after the birth! The doctor walked in 30 minutes late with a big smile on his face. I looked at him and told him, "Doc, if you worked for Domino's Pizza, this delivery would be free!" He laughed and billed me anyway.

As you can see, this second pregnancy was absolutely

supernatural! However, I am convinced that the catalyst which began the supernatural restoration was when we started thanking God not because of what happened, but in spite of what happened!

The Bible tells us, "My brethren, count it all joy when ye fall into divers temptations; Knowing this, that the trying of your faith worketh patience. But let patience have her perfect work, that ye may be perfect and entire wanting nothing" (James 1:2–4). Notice the word "count." The Greek word *hegeomai* means to calculate. The word "joy" is the Greek word *chara,* which means an inward delight, celebration, or party. The word "fall" is the Greek word *peripipto,* and it means to fall into a deep hole. The Greek word translated "test" denotes a test, trial, or temptation.

Therefore, James, by the Holy Spirit, is telling us to calculate it an inward delight, celebration or party when you fall into the deep dark hole of a test, trial, or temptation. My deep dark hole was the hole of miscarriage. What hole have you fallen in today?

First, you must know that hole didn't come from God (see James 1:13, 17). Remember that your God is not a car-wrecking, cancer-causing Creator, but a loving, life-giving Lord! Second, you must calculate it all joy. In other words, your God is greater than your hole!

Now, let's look at verse three. In order to calculate it all joy, you must know something. That the "trying of your

> *Remember that your God is not a car-wrecking, cancer-causing Creator, but a loving, life-giving Lord!*

faith works patience." The word "patience" is the powerful Greek word *hupomone*. It is a Greek compound word that comes from *hupo,* which means under, and *meno,* which means to abide. Put these together, and it connotes the ability to remain in one spot without budging. In the early church, patience was referred to as the "queen of all virtues" (love was the king). Because of all the heavy persecution the early church endured, patience was a valued commodity.

When you were little, did you ever play a game of chicken? I used to play it with my brother and friends on bicycles. You would face your friend on your bike from a distance, then pedal faster and faster as you approached one another. Whoever swerved first was the chicken. *Hupomone* draws a picture of you having a faceoff with your adversary the devil, and because you are counting it all joy, suddenly an influx of God's supernatural joy floods your human spirit. This empowers you to "pedal" faster and the devil swerves off first—he is the chicken!

Notice the phrase "but let patience" in verse four. Note that it does not say "pray for patience." I may shock your theology here, but nowhere in the New Testament does it tell us to pray for patience! The Bible clearly tells us to *let* patience. (This explains why the last time you were stuck in freeway traffic and prayed for patience, you only got more frustrated!) How do we "let" patience? The context tells us very clearly: by counting it all joy!

Please look at verse four once again, and you will find the word "perfect." This is the Greek word *telios,* and it means mature or complete. Notice the last phrase: "that you may be perfect, entire, wanting nothing." Once again, the

> *Count it all joy—*
> *not because of what*
> *happened to you,*
> *but in spite of what*
> *happened to you!*

word "perfect" is the Greek word *telios*. The word "entire" is the Greek word *holokleros*. This is a Greek compound word *holo*, which means whole, and *kleros*, which means inheritance. These two Greek words together denote "to be whole in your inheritance." The last phrase "wanting nothing" means "lacking in no area of life."

So let's put all of this together by summarizing these powerful Greek words with a picture. These verses connote a person walking along the path of God's destiny for his life when, unbeknownst to him, he falls into a deep, dark hole of a test, trial, or temptation. After falling into this hole, he immediately brushes himself off, looks up, and recognizes that God is bigger than this hole. Therefore, he can calculate it all joy! Immediately, a divine flood of supernatural energy floods his soul. He is infused with the strength to stand and watch his adversary flee like a chicken. That strength is so strong that the individual is catapulted out of the hole! The person comes out, brushes himself off once again, and begins to notice something: he is more mature than ever, whole in his inheritance (the things that biblically belong to him according to the promises of God), and lacking in no area of life!

Are you old enough to remember "The Six Million Dollar Man"? It was a TV show in which an astronaut crashes and scientists rebuild him with bionic body parts. In the TV show opening, they say, "We can rebuild him ... better than he was before. Now, he is better, stronger, faster." Next time you fall into a hole in your life, you can come out like the Six Million Dollar Man (we may have to adjust for inflation): better, stronger, and faster!

Count it all joy—not *because* of what happened to you, but *in spite* of what happened to you!

CHAPTER 6

Speak It!

Don't use your words to describe your life; use your words to design your life!

I have been married to my beautiful wife for over a quarter of a century (she doesn't like that phraseology; she says it makes her sound old. So let's just say for over 25 years). As those of you who are married will understand, you can't truly know someone until you are married to them. As you live your life together on a daily basis, you begin to discover little idiosyncrasies that will either fascinate or frustrate you.

After Anne and I got married, we moved into a little apartment in East Tennessee, and it was there that I discovered one of those little idiosyncrasies that has fascinated me for over 25 years now. I was sitting in the living room of our little apartment when I heard a faint mumbling emanating from the bedroom. I was quite intrigued, so I got up and proceeded in the direction of the indistinguishable mumbling. As I drew near the bedroom, the mumbling grew a bit louder. Still, I could not see Anne anywhere. There was only one more place to go in our diminutive apartment, and that was our bedroom closet. As I approached it, the mumbling grew ever louder. There was my beautiful new bride looking at her clothes and trying to decide what to wear, talking to herself! She was carrying on quite the conversation.

This was all very new to me because our family didn't even talk to each other, let alone ourselves. Twenty-five years later, the fascination continues. To this day, I will find my lovely wife in various rooms of our house talking to herself about the various projects she must undertake for the day.

Shortly after we married, Anne's parents came to visit their youngest daughter and the guy that stole her from them. After my new in-laws got settled into our little spare bedroom, I once again heard some faint mumbling. This time, however, it was in a much lower voice. Once again, I got up and headed towards the mumbling. I opened the door to our spare bedroom to find my father-in-law looking in his little closet and talking to himself! Truly the apple doesn't fall far from the tree—or should I say the "nut"!

The Bible tells us in Psalm 103:1–5, "Bless the Lord, O my soul: and all that is within me, bless his holy name. Bless the Lord, O my soul, and forget not all his benefits: Who forgives all thine iniquities; who heals all thy diseases; Who redeems thy life from destruction; who crowns thee with loving kindness and tender mercies; Who satisfies thy mouth with good things; so that thy youth is renewed like the eagle's."

Notice the phrase, "Bless the Lord, O my soul and all that is within me." Who is David talking to? He is talking to himself! While, granted, it may not be in the same fashion as my wife and father-in-law, I think you get the point. It is imperative that we *speak* the Word of God pertaining to joy *out loud.*

The New Testament tells us, "Rejoice in the Lord always: and again I say, Rejoice" (Philippians 4:4). Notice the apostle Paul, by the Holy Spirit, tells us once again that we must speak it to release it. As was already discussed, the

> *It is imperative that we speak the Word of God pertaining to joy out loud!*

force of joy resides within you if you are a born-again child of God (see Galatians 5:22–23). However, that powerful force of joy will do you no good unless you release it. You release it by speaking the Scriptures that pertain to joy!

This is one of my keys as to why I have not been down, discouraged, or depressed for decades. I don't use my words to *describe* my life; I use my words to *design* my life! Many mornings, particularly if I am facing a difficult time personally or ministerially, I will begin by speaking Scriptures regarding joy. I'll start with "This is the day the Lord has made, I will rejoice and be glad in it" (Psalm 118:24). Then "The joy of the Lord is my strength" (Nehemiah 8:10). Then "Rejoice in the Lord always: and again I say, rejoice" (Philippians 4:4). Again and again, I will speak the Scriptures on joy out loud. I will speak the promises of God on joy until I can sense those Scriptures flooding my soul and infusing me with strength. The more difficult the circumstances, the longer I will speak them.

> *You can partake of the divine nature of God through the divine promises of God!*

The Bible tells us in 2 Peter 1:3-4, "According as his divine power hath given unto us all things that pertain unto life and godliness, through the knowledge of him that hath called us to glory and virtue: Whereby are given unto us exceeding great and precious promises: that by these ye might be partakers of the divine nature, having escaped the corruption that is in the world through lust."

You see, you can partake of the divine nature of God through these divine promises of God. It is not God's nature to be down, depressed, or discouraged, but up, joyful, and encouraged! You can partake of His nature through His promises.

The Bible also tells us, "All scripture is given by inspiration of God and is profitable for doctrine, for reproof, for correction, for instruction in righteousness" (2 Timothy 3:16). Notice the phrase "inspiration of God." It is one Greek word *theopneustas*. This is a compound Greek word that literally means "God-breathed." If I were to blow up a balloon it would contain my breath, my very DNA. In the same vein, God's promises contain *His* very breath and DNA, and when you believe and speak the promises of God on joy, they blow His strength into you!

"But Pastor Jim, with all the negative circumstances I am presently facing, I don't *feel* like speaking anything but doom and gloom!" I learned a long time ago to let your feelings into your car, but never let them in the driver's seat. Never feel your way into acting; act your way into feeling!

> *Never feel your way into acting; act your way into feeling!*

We live in a culture that worships our feelings. Our lives, relationships, and even music revolve around our feelings. Do you remember the old song, "You lost that lovin' feeling"? Remember the old commercial jingle, "Sometimes you feel like a nut, sometimes you don't"? However, as a believer, you must understand all feelings are derived from thoughts. All thoughts come from words. Therefore, if I want to change my feelings, I must change my words, which will in turn change my thoughts, which will in turn change my feelings. Obviously, my words must line up with His Word.

Speak it! Don't use your words to *describe* your life; use your words to *design* your life!

All feelings are derived from thoughts.
All thoughts come from words.
Therefore, if I want to change my feelings,
I must change my words, which will in turn
change my thoughts, which will in turn
change my feelings.

CHAPTER 7

Repeat It!

Because we learn by repetition.
Because we learn by repetition.
Because we learn by repetition.

Very early in my ministry, in the mid-1990s, I received an opportunity to speak at a fairly large church, committing to have me teach both on Sunday morning and Sunday evening services. Now, this was extremely important to us as we had just founded World Changers Bible Institute. Anne and I were living in an apartment, and we were barely getting by month to month. This was a huge deal to us! We had this locked into our schedule for months, and we were very much looking forward to ministering.

One afternoon, we received a call from a pastoral staff member who represented this church. He spoke in a tone that clearly let me know he was doing the bidding of the pastor, but not too thrilled to share this news with me. He said, "Brother Jim"—you know when someone begins a sentence with Brother Jim you are about to have an "Oh Brother" moment—"I know we have committed to you for months that you were going to speak both Sunday morning and evening at our church. However, we have a standing arrangement with 'Brother Big' that if at any time he calls and tells us he will be in town and wants to minister, we will rearrange whatever is necessary to have him speak here at our church. Well, guess what? He has just told us he will be here on the Sunday morning you were supposed to speak. So now we are going to have him speak on Sunday morning, and you can still speak on Sunday evening."

The reason I refer to him as "Brother Big" is that I had an unfortunate run-in with him a couple of years prior. "Brother Big" is a national speaker with a great deal of renown, and he had called me out in a meeting to give what he thought was a word from the Lord. However his "word from the Lord" was completely inaccurate and, honestly, a little bit embarrassing. So needless to say, I was not a big fan of "Brother Big" to begin with—probably even less so now! I was being bumped to the much lower-attended, much less significant night service by a national minister who was not exactly at the top of my all-time favorite minister list.

When I got off that phone call, I could feel discouragement trying to crawl up my leg. I immediately went into my bathroom, looked at myself directly in the mirror, and began to encourage myself in the Lord. The Bible tells us that King David, in one of the darkest times in his life, encouraged *himself* in the Lord his God (see 1 Samuel 30:1–6). In essence, you become your own personal cheerleader! Please don't misunderstand me, I did not look in the mirror and say, "Two, four, six, eight who do I appreciate? Me, me, me!" No, when you encourage yourself *in the Lord*, you do so with the power of the Word of God.

That day when I went into my bathroom and looked in the mirror, I began to quote John 15:13, which says, "Greater love has no man than this, that a man lay down his life for his friends." If "Brother Big" could help this church more

> *When you encourage yourself in the Lord, you do so with the power of the Word of God.*

than I could, I was determined to "lay down my life" in this situation. In other words, I was going to lay down my feelings, my agenda, and even my concern with "Brother Big" if he could help this church grow in the Word of God. I quoted this powerful Scripture over and over and over again. I even grabbed myself by the ear and said out loud, "Jim, you lay down your life in this situation." It took about 20 minutes of encouraging myself in the Lord, but I could feel the discouragement crawl right back down my leg and back to the devil where it belonged! I walked out of the bathroom a free man.

The Bible says, "Rejoice in the Lord always: and *again* I say, rejoice" (Philippians 4:4). There are many times in life when you "Rejoice in the Lord," but it needs to be repeated— again, I say rejoice! Let's say you are going through a difficult situation, yet you choose to go to your local church and you leave that service brimming with joy! As you return to your home, someone cuts you off on the interstate. Even though it is his fault, this wonderful driver has the audacity to show you his "one way to Jesus" finger. It's in moments like this that you need to say, "Again, I say rejoice!"

Remember, you can't do what you don't remember, and you don't remember what is not repeated!

CHAPTER 8

Renew It!

Because you don't see life as it is; you see life as you are!

A few years ago, Anne and I took our son Johnathan to Gatlinburg, Tennessee, to celebrate his birthday. We rented a condo that had two big indoor waterslides. You know the type—it twists and turns as you travel down the slide at high rates of speed. Once you jump in, this slide is going to take you where it wants you to go whether you like it or not!

One evening, I was sitting by one of these waterslides, just watching the people jump in and slide down. I wasn't the only one watching the fun; there was a man maybe in his early seventies watching as well. After studying this situation for a while, he looked to his friends, and with a big grin on his face, he bravely told them that he was going to go down the slide. I watched him courageously climb the steps and take the plunge into the water slide. The elderly man came flying down into the exit pool. Because of all the twists and turns, he was completely disoriented. He was flailing wildly and could not determine up or down; therefore, he couldn't come up out of the water for a much needed breath of air!

> *You can't change your destination overnight, but you can change your direction overnight!*

The funny thing was that the little exit pool was only four feet deep. For a moment, I thought I was going to have to save the man from drowning in water in which he could easily stand up. Finally, the old man's head popped above the surface of the water, and he gasped for air. His eyes were rolling up and down and all around, obviously quite dizzy and disoriented. I watched his eyes slowly begin to focus, and as they did, I also saw that big silly grin return to his face. He looked over at his friends (who by this time had probably thought he had lost his mind) and said with a thick southern accent, "Let's do it again!"

Life is very similar. We seem to jump into the same "slide" over and over again, and it keeps spitting us out at the same place over and over again. We become very disoriented and swear we'll never put ourselves in that position again. However, just like that old man, we find ourselves saying, "Let's do it again!"

The Bible tells us in 2 Corinthians 10:4–5, "For the weapons of our warfare are not carnal, but mighty through God to the pulling down of strongholds; Casting down imaginations, and every high thing that exalteth itself against the knowledge of God, and bringing into captivity every thought to the obedience of Christ."

The Greek word for "strongholds" denotes a castle or fortification. So many good-hearted people in the Body of Christ teach that this is referring to demonic strongholds. However, context does not support that at all.

Rather, notice the word "imaginations" in verse five. This is the Greek word *logismos* where we get our English word "logic" from. The Greek word means reasonings or logic. God is certainly not against us being reasonable or logical. I personally wish a few more Christians would use a little more logic. Some flaky Christians are what I call "Star Trek Christians"; they boldly go where the Bible has never gone before! However when our own logic or reason contradicts the Bible, go with the Bible.

Also, notice the phrase "taking captive every thought." This is not talking about taking the devil captive. The context here is referring to the mind and our process of thinking. Thus, a biblical stronghold is simply a mindset or way of thinking. Like the waterslide, it takes us in a predetermined direction and spits us out at the same place every time! Strongholds can be either positive or negative depending on what "slide" you jump in. They can either lock God out and lock the devil in, or lock the devil out and lock God in!

One of our family's favorite vacation spots is a beautiful beach location where you can rent bicycles for the duration of your stay. This island has bike paths woven throughout, and on one of the bike paths, there is a groove that is worn into the middle of this sidewalk that is almost exactly the same size as a bike tire. If you make the mistake of entering this little groove in the sidewalk, you can't get out without wrecking your bike. Once in this groove, you are locked in, and it will take you to the same place every time.

Now you can understand why you repeat certain negative behaviors that seem to be ruining your life. You swear you'll never yell at your spouse again, but when presented with a similar set of circumstances, here you go again, losing your temper and once again yelling at your wife. You swear you'll never view that pornography again, but when presented with a similar set of circumstances, here you go again, viewing something that always leads to overwhelming guilt, robbing you of your potential and ruining intimacy with your wife. You swear you'll never date a "bad boy" again, but when presented with a similar set of circumstances, here you go again, going back to the same type of abusive men over and over again.

You say to yourself, "What was I thinking?" Without truly knowing it, you answered your own question. The answer can truly be found in *what* you were *thinking*!

The Bible tells us, "And be not conformed to this world; but be ye transformed by the renewing of your mind, that ye may prove what is that good, and acceptable, and perfect, will of God" (Romans 12:2). The word "transformed" is the Greek word *metamorphao*, from which we get our English word "metamorphosis." It is a compound Greek word that is derived from two Greek words: *meta*, which means to change, and *morph*, which means shape. Put these two Greek words together, and it means to change shape. Much like in metamorphosis when the ugly caterpillar changes into the beautiful butterfly!

In this verse, Paul, by the Holy Spirit, is telling us our life changes shape and goes from something ugly to something beautiful if we will renew our minds to the Word of God. The Bible

> *You don't see life as it is; you see life as you are.*

gives us a powerful principle in a phrase found in Proverbs 23:7, "As a man thinks in his heart, so is he." In other words, if you have limburger cheese on your mustache, all of life will stink! You can go to the bedroom and the bedroom will stink. You can go to your living room and the living room will stink. You can even go outside and the great outdoors will stink! Why? Because wherever you go, there you are!

Remember, you don't see life as it is; you see life as you are. That's why if you are ever going to change your life, you **must** change the way you are *thinking*. You must create new biblical strongholds. What you continually mind, you will eventually find. If you win the battlefield for the mind, you will win the battlefield for life!

As mentioned earlier, I used to be frequently and easily depressed, and now I have not been discouraged or depressed for decades. Many years ago, I was determined to jump in the joy "slide" by renewing my mind to His Word on the subject of joy. Now, every time discouraging or depressing circumstances come my way, my "slide" spits me out at a place of joy!

You see, once a giant snowball starts rolling down a steep hill, it is very difficult to stop. However, if you'll renew your "snowball" to God's Word on joy (or whatever area in which you need "stronghold changing"), you can have an avalanche of His strength! The joy of the Lord is your strength (Nehemiah 8:10).

I know this is America and we want microwave maturity in an instant. However, this is going to take some daily and diligent renewing of the mind. Remember, you can't change your destination overnight, but you can change your direction overnight!

So come on, renew it! That way you can start seeing life from your *position*, not from your *condition*.

CHAPTER 9

Praise It!

Because praise is <u>to</u> God, but <u>for</u> us.

My hobby is fishing for shark. (I know, I have issues!) Whether from the shore, a boat, or using a kayak, I have enjoyed fishing for shark for approximately 20 years now I've caught well over a thousand sharks. For many years, I had a fishing boat captain that I would regularly charter, and throughout the years, he and I would banter back and forth about catching a tiger shark. Our conversation was playful at first as tiger sharks are man eaters and fairly rare. Catching a tiger shark is considered a once-in-a-lifetime event.

As the years went by, our tiger shark discussion began to take on a more serious tone until I finally booked a trip with my favorite captain solely for the purpose of catching a tiger shark. My captain brought special equipment with him: a huge rod and reel combo designed specifically for very large fish.

It took us about 40 minutes to get to the fishing destination, where we anchored over a submerged wreck. We had not been fishing more than just 20 minutes when the line on his giant reel began to sing out. (To all you fishermen reading this, you know what a beautiful sound that can be. I have asked my wife Anne, who is the praise and worship leader at Joy Church, to somehow incorporate this beautiful sound into our worship—she has yet to take me up on this!)

My captain looked at me and said, "You know what you have on, don't you?!" It was the highly sought-after tiger shark! The battle was on. I would reel and make some progress, and then the shark would make a run and take back all the progress I had gained. The ocean was very rough that day, and we were fishing in the midst of eight-foot wave swells when suddenly it hit me—full blown sea sickness! If you have ever experienced severe sea sickness, you know it's true when I say it is the worst feeling ever. As an Ohio State football fan, I would not wish this upon a Michigan Wolverine (well, let me pray about that)!

What a dilemma... I was in the midst of catching the fish of my dreams, and I knew I was about to chum the water with my breakfast! I had a very difficult choice: I could either stop fishing and hand the rod to the captain, or I could keep fishing and vomit in his boat. I chose the latter. I simply turned my head to the side, violently threw up in my friend's boat, and kept on fishing!

After a long battle, I finally reeled the shark all the way

to the boat. The first mate looked at the captain and said, "Now, that guy's a true fisherman!" Then I saw the look on his face when he realized he was going to have to clean the boat deck. When we finally arrived back at the dock and I stepped on dry, steady ground, I don't think I had ever been more thankful in my life!

Biblically speaking, if we want to enjoy our lives, it is vital that we be people who live a lifestyle of thanking and praising God! The Word of God tells us in Acts 16:23–26, "And when they had laid many stripes upon them, they cast them into prison, charging the jailer to keep them safely: Who, having received such a charge, thrust them into the inner prison, and made their feet fast in the stocks. And at midnight Paul and Silas prayed, and sang praises unto God: and the prisoners heard them. And suddenly there was a great earthquake, so that the foundations of the prison were shaken: and immediately all the doors were opened, and every one's bands were loosed."

> *If we want to enjoy our lives, it is vital that we be people who live a lifestyle of thanking and praising God!*

Here, Paul and Silas were in a place called Macedonia, and as they were going to prayer one day, they met a woman much like a modern day fortune teller. This woman, the Bible says, was possessed with a demon. She was a slave that brought her master a lot of money through her demonic craft. Paul cast the spirit out in the name of Jesus, which angered the fortune teller's owner because they saw a significant source of their income was now gone. These evil owners brought Paul and Silas to the local magistrates, and there the magistrates ordered that Paul and Silas be beaten and sent to prison. (See Acts 16:16–23).

They were thrown into the "inner prison." This was a very deep, dark portion of the prison, at the time reserved for only the worst criminals. Notice, however, at the darkest place and in the darkest hour, Paul and Silas "prayed and *sang praise* unto God". You know the rest of the story: the "foundations of the prison were shaken and immediately all the doors were opened and everyone's bands were loosed." This is where "jailhouse rock" first originated!

The Bible tells us in Hebrews 13:15, "By him therefore let us offer the sacrifice of praise to God continually, that is, the fruit of our lips giving thanks to his name." In the Old Covenant, they offered animal sacrifices. In the New Covenant, we offer the *sacrifice of praise*. In any sacrifice, something always has to die. In the Old Covenant, it was some sort of sacrificial animal. In the New Covenant, we must sacrifice our negative emotions. To offer the sacrifice of praise, our negative emotions must die.

Like Paul and Silas, when we are in the midst of deep, dark, negative circumstances, whatever they may be, it is *imperative* we give God praise. The most important time to give God praise is when you *least* feel like it. It is a sacrifice! You must plunge the proverbial sword of God's Word into your negative feelings and offer to God the sacrifice of praise: the fruit of your lips giving thanks to God!

> *The most important time to give God praise is when you least feel like it.*

Please don't misunderstand me, I don't want you to misplace your thanksgiving and praise. The Bible says, "Giving thanks always for all things unto God and the Father in the name of our Lord Jesus Christ" (Ephesians 5:20). Now if you simply study the Bible casually, you could misinterpret that verse. You could think we are supposed to thank God for all things, even things the devil does. Does this verse mean "all things," period, or "all things" that God does?

Remember, Scripture can't be isolated and taken out of context. The best way to interpret Scripture is in context and in light of the entire Bible. You must compare Scripture with Scripture (2 Corinthians 13:1). If you look further in Ephesians 5:24, Paul, by the Holy Spirit, discusses marriage, telling us, "Therefore as the church is subject unto Christ; so let the woman be to their own husbands in every thing." Once again, is this everything period or everything biblical?

Should wives submit to pornography to spice up the marriage? God forbid! Should wives submit to helping their husbands cheat on their taxes? Of course not! Clearly, Paul is talking about submitting to everything *biblical*. Once someone in authority steps outside of their biblical bounds, they lose that authority in that area because we all must submit to God and His Word, which, of course, is the highest authority. In the same vein, we should not be thankful for "all things," but only "all things" that God does!

> *The Bible tells us to be thankful in everything, not for everything.*

In contrast, the Bible says, "In everything give thanks for this is the will of God in Christ Jesus concerning you" (1 Thessalonians 5:15). Here, the Bible tells us to be thankful *in* everything, not *for* everything. Therefore, you should be thankful to God in the midst of the car wreck, but certainly not *for* the car wreck. Why? Because God did not cause the car wreck. Remember that your God is not a car-wrecking, cancer-causing Creator, but a loving, life-giving Lord!

Let's say that you went out of town, and while you were gone, I decided to bless you and surprise you by mowing your lawn, taking out your garbage, and cleaning your gutters. Upon your return, you notice all three of these things and decide to write me a thank you note. "Dear Pastor Jim," you write, "thank you for mowing my lawn, taking out my garbage, cleaning my gutters, and killing my cat!" When I receive this thank you note, I am incredulous! I immediately call you and let you know "While I certainly did mow the lawn, take out your garbage, and clean the gutters, I would *never* kill your cat! Please don't thank me for something I did not do!"

If we are going to live a joyful life, full of thanksgiving and praise, we must also be aware of one of the devil's biggest tricks. He's been doing it since the Garden of Eden. When we hear the term "garden," we think in terms of some little patch of dirt with tomato plants growing in it. However, the biblical Garden of Eden was much more like a park, filled with probably hundreds, maybe thousands, of trees.

So what does the devil do? He tries to get Adam and Eve to focus on the *one* tree they can't have (see Genesis 3:1–6). The enemy still does this today in our local churches. There are so many good churches filled with so many good "trees," yet the devil endeavors to get well-meaning, church-going Christians to focus on the one thing the church doesn't have. I see the same thing in marriages today. Did you know that statistics tell us that when a husband or wife leaves his or her spouse, they are happy with about 80% of their marriage? However, they leave their spouse to find that elusive 20%. The problem with that thinking is that everybody has a 20%, and some have 30%, 40%, or more! The grass is always greener on the other side until you have to mow it.

My wife and I have made a list of attributes that we like about each other, and many times over the years, when I pull out my list and Anne pulls out her 75-foot scroll, we focus on and we are thankful for all the trees in the garden we *can* have!

As an avid fisherman, I had always desired a fishing boat. Nothing fancy, just functional enough to catch some shark. Many years ago, my wife and I prayed about owning a boat. We began to put money away towards this goal. We saved for many years, regularly putting small amounts of finances away toward its purchase. Finally, the day came when I purchased my boat. We hooked that beautiful boat up to my SUV, and I began to drive it home. I am a very happy person as it is, but I think my smile was ear to ear on that eventful day! As I was driving home, I noticed a truck pulling a similar boat, only it was upgraded two or three levels. It's amazing how quickly my smile began to diminish as I twisted my neck to catch one last look at the better boat!

Awareness leads to covetousness. I never coveted that upgrade until I was made aware of it! The Bible says in Proverbs 27:20, "Hell and destruction are never full; so the eyes of man are never satisfied." It also tells us, "Wilt thou set thine eyes upon that which is not? For riches certainly make themselves wings; they fly away as an eagle toward heaven" (Proverbs 23:5).

I discovered a long time ago that the key to being a

joy-filled person of thanksgiving and praise is to focus on what you do have, not what you don't! Focus on how far you have come, not how far you have to go!

Remember, praise is *to* God, but it's *for* you!

The key to being a joy-filled person of thanksgiving and praise is to focus on what you do have, not what you don't!

Focus on how far you have come, not how far you have to go!

CHAPTER 10

Laugh at It!

If you don't believe God has a sense of humor, simply look in the mirror!

Many years ago, in our old church building, my office was directly across from the children's ministry. There I would frequently see a young lady who worked as a children's greeter. Whenever we saw each other, we would greet one another, and then I would say, "I like your nose ring."

We have a church that emphasizes the heart (see 1 Samuel 16:7) and de-emphasizes tattoos, nose rings, etc. Sometimes, people can feel a little self-conscious around their pastor, so I will endeavor to make them feel at ease.

Week after week, I would greet her, encourage her, and tell her, "I like your nose ring." Finally, after about four separate "nose ring encouragements," this gracious young lady mustered up all the courage she had and said, "Pastor, it's not a nose ring—it's a mole." At that point all you can do is grovel and thank God that He has a sense of humor!

The Bible tells us, "A merry heart doeth good like a medicine: but a broken spirit drieth the bones" (Proverbs 17:22). After more than three decades of ministry, I have discovered that if you are really going to enjoy your life, it is absolutely vital to have a sense of humor! Please don't mistake me, I take my relationship with God and the responsibility I have to His call on my life very seriously. As a matter of fact, I am probably one of the most responsible people you will ever meet. Remember, God wants us to be *care-free*, just not *careless*! (See 1 Peter 5:7).

> *If you are really going to enjoy your life, it is absolutely vital to have a sense of humor!*

However, I have learned to have a sense of humor about almost everything—including myself! When I was a young man, I would get embarrassed very easily, and that carried over into my early years of Christianity. This caused me to be quite insecure as I walked through many embarrassing situations in my life. However, the Bible tells us, "Don't be ashamed of the gospel of Christ for it is the power of God unto salvation..." (Romans 1:16). Paul, by the Holy Spirit, knew that if we were embarrassed by the Gospel, we would never be effective witnesses for our Lord.

Remember, when you are embarrassed, you are controlled. Embarrassment brought on by personal insecurities is fear-based. The only cure for fear of any type is a deep revelation of God's love for you! The Bible says in 1 John 4:18, "There is no fear in love; but

> *The only cure for fear of any type is a deep revelation of God's love for you!*

perfect love casteth out fear: because fear hath torment. He that feareth is not made perfect in love." The Greek word translated "casts out" is the word *ballo*, which means to throw out.

When I was 19 years old, before I was born again, I used to check IDs at a bar. One time, I had to throw out a very unruly patron (which is a nice, Christian way of saying a drunken idiot). This belligerent man was not at all cooperative in his departure (which is another nice, Christian way of saying the idiot wouldn't leave!). I literally had to pick him up and carry him out of the bar.

As I was carrying him through the bar foyer, he latched onto a pillar and wouldn't let go. Since my arms and hands were preoccupied with carrying him, I couldn't pry his hands loose. I simply had to pull on his entire body until he acquiesced and let go. Finally, I was able to get him out of the foyer, and I don't think he ever came back!

Fear and fear-based insecurity is similar. The more you immerse yourself in how much God loves you, His love begins to pick up fear to cast it out of your life. Though it endeavors to hold on and clutch your soul tightly, it will eventually let go and be forever cast out of your life!

> *Learn from it.*
> *Laugh at it.*
> *Let it go!*

The Bible also tells us that we are "accepted in the beloved" (Ephesians 1:6). The word "accepted" means highly favored. In Christ (a term that simply means how God sees you because of what Christ has done for you), we are highly favored! When you are accepted by the Best, who cares about the rest? When you see yourself "in Christ," you can respond to your situations from your *position*, not your *condition*!

The more you discern just how much God loves you and how He sees you in Christ, the more secure you will become. When you are secure, embarrassment will begin to melt away. Now, when you make a mistake (as we all undoubtedly do) you can simply laugh at yourself. Learn from it, laugh at it, and then let it go!

One of my favorite people is my Executive Pastor. He has served the Lord faithfully by my side for nearly three decades. I remember speaking at a pastors' conference in Trinidad, and he was listening intently in the audience. Many of these conferences can tend to be a bit stuffy; pastors can be some of the hardest people to preach to, since many of them have "heard it all."

Suddenly, as I was preaching, one of the pastors tumbled over backwards in his chair. To my chagrin, I discovered it was my own faithful Executive Pastor! He had tipped his chair back, and the legs of the chair had crumbled underneath him, resulting in him flipping over backwards in his chair. He looked like a turtle flipped upside down, trying to get back to his feet—all I saw was his legs high in the air kicking and flailing wildly! The other thing I could see was my Missions Director (who has also been with me for nearly three decades) doubled over laughing uncontrollably at the plight of my Executive Pastor!

Whenever this story comes up (and my Missions Director and I make sure that it does), my Executive Pastor laughs at this situation because he is secure in God's love for him. It's easy to laugh when everything is going right. It's important to laugh when everything is going wrong.

> *It's easy to laugh when everything is going right.*
>
> *It's important to laugh when everything is going wrong.*

If you want to truly enjoy your life, you must remember the power of laughter. Laughter gives you perspective. It also reminds your enemy he is defeated. When he gives you his best shot and all you do is laugh, it will discourage him!

Many decades ago, before I met Jesus, I had a very violent temper. Many times, my rage would outweigh my common sense. I was in a bar one evening and a giant of a man began to hassle my friend. This behemoth, an off-duty policeman, stood about 6'6" and weighed at least 280 pounds of trained muscle. I was so angry with this huge fellow for mistreating my friend that I hauled off and hit him square in the head! This big policeman simply fell back a few feet and then immediately jumped back into my face! My best shot barely fazed him. In essence, he "laughed off" my best shot, and I can promise you, I was discouraged.

Laughter has a healing power in it (see Proverbs 17:22). I recall reading about a man who had terminal cancer and only had a short time to live. He reasoned that since he only had a little time left on this planet, he would rent all the funny movies and shows he could find and enjoy the remaining time he had left here. From his hospital bed he watched show after show. The doctors and nurses on his wing would hear loud belly laughs coming from his room day after day after day!

After about a month of this continual laughter gushing forth from a merry heart, he was re-tested. They discovered this jovial man had absolutely no trace of cancer in his body—he literally laughed his way to health!

If we are to truly enjoy our Christian journey, we have to learn to lighten up and laugh a little! If you don't think God has a sense of humor, just look in the mirror!

CHAPTER 11

Don't Lose It!

Anything gained must be maintained.

I truly love my wife, Anne; she is my best friend! I remember our honeymoon like it was yesterday: a marvelous vacation at a beach in South Carolina. One afternoon Anne was simply wading in the ocean when she was stung by a jellyfish. If you have never been stung by a jellyfish, you don't know the acute pain they can cause. My lovely wife came running on the shore in quite a bit of agony. There are a number of things that can minimize the pain of a jellyfish sting. One of them is to simply go back into the ocean and let the saltwater dry out the sting. Of course, the down side of that cure is the ocean—it's where the jellyfish live!

Being the encouraging, inspirational minister that I am, I proceeded to give my new bride a pep talk about getting back up on the proverbial horse, or she may never ride again! It was one of the most eloquent, thoughtful, inspiring "sermons" I have ever given. It had three powerful points, and it included everything but an altar call. My beautiful bride was not all that thrilled with me or my "sermon". However, reluctantly, she slowly shuffled her way back to the ocean with me.

A few short minutes later, I suddenly felt a searing pain slicing through my hamstring. I winced in horrible pain and ran back on to the shore! I had been sliced by the barb in the tail of a sting ray. It is unlikely you've ever been stuck by a sting ray, but it makes a jellyfish sting seem like you are being tickled. I remembered the "inspirational" message I had just given my wife and was regretting every single word of that stupid sermon. I did not want to go back in that ocean because it was clearly filled with demon-possessed aquatic monsters!

Throughout the entire ordeal, my sweet wife was not too happy with me. You see, we were still married but briefly "out of fellowship." The Bible tells us in 1 John 1:3–4, "That which we have seen and heard declare we unto you, that ye also may have fellowship with us: and truly our fellowship is with the Father, and with his Son Jesus Christ. And these things write we unto you, that your joy may be full."

The word "fellowship" in verse three is the Greek word *koinonia*. It means to have common union with—or, to be in fellowship. John, by the Holy Spirit, is writing this to us so our joy would be full. That tells us that if we don't understand these truths, figuratively speaking, our joy can "leak."

The Bible talks about two different types of Christians: spiritual and carnal (see Galatians 6:1 and 1 Corinthians 3:1–3). Simply put, those in fellowship with Him and those out of fellowship with Him. Please don't misunderstand me; I am not talking about being out of a *relationship* with Him. Thank God, our salvation is safe and secure in Christ (see John 11:28, Ephesians 1:13, 2:8–9, Colossians 3:3, Titus 1:2). I'm talking about being out of *fellowship* with Him.

The Bible has many synonyms for a believer who is out of fellowship with Christ: "carnal," "salt that lost its savor" (Luke 14:24), a "candle hid under a bushel" (Mark 4:21), a "prodigal" (Luke 15:11–32), "sleeping" (Ephesians 5:14), "dead while they live" (1 Timothy 5:6), and "walking in darkness" (1 John 1:6). In fellowship, we are controlled by the Spirit (see Galatians 5:16). Out of fellowship, we are controlled by the flesh.

Again, please don't mistake me. You have the joy of the Lord in your spirit the entire time you are "out of fellowship" with God. This is the fruit of the Spirit that God has dropped in your human spirit. That joy has been in you since you gave your life to Jesus (see Galatians 5:22), but it does you no good unless it floods your soul (your mind, will, and emotions). Like a faucet does you no good when you close off the nozzle, joy in your sprit is shut off from your soul when you are out of fellowship with God.

The Bible tells us in 1 John 1:5–9, "This then is the message which we have heard of him, and declare unto you, that God is light, and in him is no darkness at all. If we say that we have fellowship with him, and walk in darkness, we lie, and do not the truth: But if we walk in the light, as he is in the light, we have fellowship one with another, and the blood of Jesus Christ his Son cleanses us from all sin. If we say that we have no sin, we deceive ourselves and the truth is not in us. If we confess our sins, he is faithful and just to forgive us our sin, and to cleanse us from all unrighteousness."

> *It's not what you do when you sin that counts. It's what you do after you sin.*

Notice in verses 6 and 8 the phrase "if we say." Notice the contrast with verse 9 where it says "if we confess." We get in trouble when we "say." When we sin and we say, "Well, everyone is doing that" or "The culture accepts this," we get into the slippery slope of self-justification. Adam, after he sinned in the Garden of Eden, did the same thing when he sewed together fig leaves to cover himself after he sinned. However, when we "confess" is when we get back into fellowship with our loving heavenly Father.

The word "confess" is the Greek word *homologeo*. It is a compound Greek word deriving from *homo*, which means same, and *logeo* which means word. Put these two Greek words together, and it means "to say the same thing as". In other words, when I want to get rid of my sin, I say the

> *Grace is not the power of God to overlook sin. Grace is the power of God to overcome sin.*

same thing as God. If He calls it a sin, yet the culture calls it an addiction, I agree with God and say the same thing He does: it is a sin. So when I confess and forsake my sin, He is faithful and just to forgive and cleanse me from all unrighteousness. I am immediately back into fellowship with God, my "faucet of joy" is turned back on, and it can once again flood my soul!

While King David lived in the Old Covenant and therefore was not born again and did not have the fruit of the Spirit inside him, we can still use him as an example to us in the New Covenant (see 1 Corinthians 10:11). As you know, David committed adultery with Bathsheba, lied, and had her husband Uriah the Hittite killed to cover up his sin (see 2 Samuel 11–12). He spent about a year out of fellowship with God.

Finally, God sent Nathan the prophet to David. Nathan shared a parabolic story of two men (see 2 Samuel 12:1–4). David was so deceived that he had no clue that this story was about him (see 2 Samuel 12:5–6). Over all my years of ministry I have discovered that people who are out of fellowship with God will "Amen" enthusiastically to sermons about sins they are involved in!

> *Don't run from God —run to God.*

Finally, David realized that he was playing the starring role in this spiritual play, and he said, "...I have sinned against the Lord..." (2 Samuel 12:13). This, in essence, is David taking advantage of 1 John 1:9. In Psalm 51, David recounts this situation and says, "Restore unto me the joy of my salvation" (Psalm 51:12). For an entire year, David's joy had been "leaking," and now that he had confessed and forsaken his sin (see Proverbs 28:13), his joy had returned!

The Bible tells us, "And it shall come to pass as soon as the soles of the feet of the priests that bear the ark of the Lord, the Lord of all the earth, shall rest in the waters of Jordan, that the waters of Jordan shall be cut off from the waters that come down from above; and they shall stand upon an heap. And it came to pass, when the people removed from their tents, to pass over Jordan, and the priests bearing the ark of the covenant before the people; And as they that bare the ark were come unto Jordan, and the feet of the priests that bare the ark were dipped in the brim of the water, (for Jordan overfloweth all his banks all the time of harvest,) That the waters which came down from above stood and rose up upon an heap very far from the city of Adam, that is beside Zaretan: and those that came down toward the sea of the plain even the salt sea, failed, and were cut off: and the people passed over right against Jericho. And the priests that bare the ark of the covenant of the Lord stood firm on dry ground in the midst of Jordan, and all the Israelites passed over on dry ground, until all the people were passed clean over Jordan" (Joshua 3:13–17).

The children of Israel, as they made their exodus from Egypt (a type of sin and bondage), and then later into their Canaan (a type of abundant life in Christ after you've been born again), had to cross two bodies of water. As they left Egypt, they crossed the Red Sea (a type of the blood of Jesus). At that body of water they were slaves and all they had to do was "... stand still and see the salvation of the Lord" (see Exodus 14:13). The Red Sea split, and they crossed it. Then, as Joshua was leading the children of Israel into Canaan they came to their second body of water: the Jordan River. The high priests were required to put their feet into the water before the water split and they could cross it.

In type and shadow, this has a powerful New Testament meaning to us. Before we were born again, we were slaves, in bondage to sin. When we invited Jesus in our hearts, we were not required to confess our sins. Our confession as sinners was "Jesus, be my Lord" (see Romans 10:9–10). As a slave, I had no power over sin, and therefore, in order to "cross the blood of Jesus" into my salvation, I simply had to receive this by grace through faith (see Ephesians 2:8–9). I only had to "stand still" and see the salvation of the Lord. However, now that I am saved, the Bible says I am a priest (see 1 Peter 2:9), and therefore, as I press into my abundant life in Christ, when I sin, I am responsible to put my "feet into the river." Not my entire body, as I am not out of *relationship* with Him, but simply out of *fellowship* with Him. I simply dip my feet into the waters of 1 John 1:9, and He is faithful and just to forgive and cleanse me from all unrighteousness!

Admit it, quit it, then forget it!

Notice the phrase from Joshua 3:16, "That the water which came down from above stood and rose up upon an heap very far from the city of Adam..." This tells us that the sins of your ancestors are not stronger than the blood of Jesus Christ. This is why I don't believe in what is so prominently taught by so many in the Body of Christ: generational curses. I believe in generational *choices* (see Deuteronomy 30:19). *I believe nothing and no one can stop you from fulfilling all God has called you to do.* If that doesn't make your joy full, then I don't know what will!

Allow me to give you nine principles from 1 John 1:9 as you "come to your senses" and return to fellowship with the Lord:

1. It's not what you do *when* you sin that counts. It's what you do *after* you sin.

2. Don't run from God—run *to* God.

3. When you confess your sin is not when He found out about it.

4. This is not a license to sin, but a license to serve.

5. Grace is not the power of God to *overlook* sin. Grace is the power of God to *overcome* sin.

6. Admit it, quit it, then forget it!

7. Don't nurse it or rehearse it. Disperse it!

8. Learn from it, laugh at it, let it go!

9. Never let *what you did* define you; always let *what He did for you* define you!

The Bible tells us that we are new creations in Christ Jesus. "Old things are passed away; behold, all things are become new" (2 Corinthians 5:17). You are a new creature on the inside, in your born-again human spirit. God sees you as a spiritual superman/woman on the inside. Faster than a speeding demon, more powerful than the deacon board, and able to leap Sister Bucket Mouth in a single bound! Yet too many of us are walking around like Clark Kent, clumsily tripping over our own two feet, walking around in darkness and out of fellowship with God, wondering why we have no strength in our lives.

Jump into the phone booth of I John 1:9, and come flying out filled with the joy of the Lord that is your strength! Stop leakin' it! Remember, what is *gained* must be *maintained*.

CHAPTER 12

Make It!

Because you can't live your life from there, you must live your life from here!

When I first gave my life to Jesus, I was a student at the University of Tennessee. I lived in some pretty antiquated off-campus apartments. It was there that I met Mary, an 84-year-old widow with very little money and no car. I met her one day as she was walking past my apartment on the way to buy some groceries. As a brand-new Christian, I was very zealous for the Lord and would regularly reach out to people in conversation, hoping to eventually share the Gospel with them.

I struck up a conversation with Mary and we had an excellent rapport with one another. Initially, I did not discuss anything too heavy with Mary since I was hoping to develop a relationship with her. I wanted to eventually win her to

Christ! As the days went by, I would actually look for Mary in order to encourage her. She was sweet, funny, and quite an engaging woman. I would see Mary on a very regular basis, but one day, after not seeing her for two weeks, I asked my neighbor, "Have you seen Mary?"

"Didn't you hear?" he replied.

"Hear what?" I retorted.

"Mary was walking somewhere when she was hit by a car and was killed."

After the initial shock of this sudden announcement wore off, waves of guilt began to crash over my soul. You see, I knew God was clearly telling me, as a new believer, to share the good news of Jesus Christ with Mary. I had good intentions, but to be honest, I procrastinated long enough that I never took advantage of the opportunity. As far as I knew, sweet little Mary was in Hell.

As a young believer, this truly rocked my world. I asked God to forgive me, but guilt and condemnation seemed like it was being shoveled upon my heart until I began to feel buried under the weight of it. Finally after a couple weeks of vacationing on a major guilt trip, the warmth of God's love began to minister to me. I knew if I was ever going to be a productive part of the Kingdom of God I needed to free myself from the guilt associated with past sin.

The Bible tells us in 1 John 1:9, "If we confess our sin, he is faithful and just to forgive us our sin; and cleanse us from all unrighteousness." There are two major parts of that powerful verse. First, forgiveness. I had readily received it, but notice the second part, lesser known, "cleansing from all unrighteousness." This is freedom from all guilt associated with past sin. In other words, if you have confessed and forsaken a sin but you are continually rehearsing it in your head, chances are you have received your forgiveness but not yet your cleansing from all unrighteousness.

While the idea of Mary being tormented in Hell is still a horrific thought, I knew I had to make my life constructive once again. You will never be productive or constructive in the Kingdom of God mired under a mountain of guilt (see Hebrews 9:14). 1 John 1:9 is certainly not a license to sin, but it is a license to serve.

The Bible tells us something very powerful in 1 Thessalonians 5:16: "Rejoice evermore." At first glance this seems to be a cute little verse that you can put over your fireplace on a plaque that you purchased at your local Christian bookstore. However, it is one of the most powerful verses in all the Bible if we are to truly enjoy our life and not just endure it.

The word "evermore," in the Greek language, could be translated *from this time on*. More simply put, from here. We could paraphrase this verse and say, "Rejoice *from here*." Remember, if you are to live a joy-filled life, you can't live your life from there. You must live your life *from here*.

Here are five simple things you must remember to live your life in a joyful, constructive fashion:

1. We all have "woulda, shoulda, couldas."

2. If "ifs" and "buts" were candy and nuts, we'd all have a merry Christmas!

3. There are three emotions that will keep you stuck in the past: guilt, regret, and self-pity.

4. God has a plan for wherever you land.

5. One thing I discovered about yesterday: it ended last night!

One of the things I love about 1 Thessalonians 5:16 is that the Greek reads "Rejoice *from this point on*." Every time you look at that verse, it updates itself. While we all have reasons we could be depressed, none of us have excuses. Every time I look at this verse, it tells me, from this point on, rejoice!

In other words, you could have had a really lousy last year but from this point on, rejoice! You could have had a really lousy last month, but from this point on, rejoice! You could have had a really lousy last week, but from this point on, rejoice! You could have had a really lousy day, but from this point on, rejoice! You could have had a really lousy last hour, but from this point on, rejoice! You could have had a really lousy last minute (I don't see how that is possible considering you have been reading this book!), but from this point on, rejoice! We must live our lives from here!

After teaching about this, someone in my church wanted to share with me an awesome story. He, like his pastor, had a pretty rough past. During his life before Jesus, he had gotten many tattoos—many of them skulls, and one of them a naked woman. He had come to Joy Church for a few months and understood that God was a God of hearts and was not looking at his tattoos. But he knew his wife was! Since he could not have them removed he decided to go *from here*. He went back to the tattoo parlor and had the artist put clothes on the naked woman and a scripture over every skull!

In life, sometimes you are the pigeon, and sometimes you are the statue. But you can't go back and un-ring certain bells. You can't unscramble eggs. Rejoice from this point on because you can't live your life from there. You must live your life *from here!*

God has a plan for wherever you land.

CHAPTER 13

Don't Let People Steal It!

If you are continually getting kicked in the rear, chances are you are out front leading!

"Shameful", "silly", and "unintelligent" were just three words used by a Chicago newspaper to describe a presidential speech given in 1865. This critique was directed at Abraham Lincoln for his Gettysburg Address!

Moses, at great personal risk, obeyed God and put his life on the line to free the children of Israel. To Pharaoh, he uttered the famous words, "Let my people go." As the children of Israel trod through the wilderness, they primarily did three things: ate manna, ate quail, and complained— primarily to leadership. In retrospect, Moses might have wanted to modify his command to "Let *some* of my people go!" Or even better, "Let only Joshua and Caleb go!"

As you can see, if you have been criticized or persecuted you are in good company. Joseph, a truly pure man of God, was accused of rape (see Genesis 39:7–20). Paul, Apostle to the Gentiles, was accused of being a cult leader (see Acts 24:5). Jesus, the Son of the living God, was accused of having a devil (see Matthew 12:24)! The Bible tells us, "All that will live godly in Christ Jesus shall suffer persecution" (2 Timothy 3:12).

> *Never allow what critics say about you change what you believe about yourself.*

People will always fight what they do not understand. Many people want what you have, but they don't want to do *what you did* to have what you have. So rather than do what you did to get what you have, they would rather run you down! Many times, when you are *in step* with God, you will be *out of step* with people. That's why, when it comes to people, we must love quickly but trust slowly (see John 2:24).

We are all human, and everybody longs to belong, so I will share with you three ways to never be criticized:

1. Say nothing!

2. Do nothing!

3. Be nothing!

There are three types of people in life: eagles, crows, and chickens. Chickens stay on the ground and cluck (gossip). Crows are loud and annoying and desire to re-direct you from God's dream. Eagles simply soar above them both and rise above it all. They see and fulfill things from God that others will never understand. Chickens and crows will always resent what they cannot master. Throughout history, eagles have always had their name tarnished by chickens and crows.

Jesus was continually vilified by the religious ruling class of the day. However, He never begged anyone to believe Him. He knew integrity can't just be verbalized; it must be observed over time. Jesus didn't just look good; He was good. Jesus didn't strive to have a good reputation; He simply had character. Never allow what critics say about you change what you believe about yourself. Critics (chickens and crows) are disappointed, disillusioned, offended, hurt, and religious people!

Don't get me wrong; we must all be teachable (Proverbs 9:7–9). Leaders are learners. Don't be a know-it-all; be a learn-it-all! The more I know, the more I know I need to know. The key to being teachable is recognizing the source. Reject critics, but receive correction. Criticism comes from a critic, but correction comes from a mentor.

> *Reject critics, but receive correction.*
>
> *Criticism comes from a critic, but correction comes from a mentor.*

Here's how to recognize the difference:

- Criticism is deadly. Correction gives life.

- Criticism points out flaws. Correction points out potential.

- Criticism tells you the truth. Correction tells you the truth in love.

Mentors are shortcuts. They can teach you in 30 minutes what has taken them a lifetime to learn. There are three ways to learn in life:

1. Your failures: good
2. Others' failures: better
3. Others' successes: best

When correction comes from a mentor, you can see their advice already working in them (see Matthew 7:1–5). I don't need parental advice from someone with no children. I don't need marital advice from the single guy on FarmersOnly.com. I don't need financial advice from someone who is broke!

Biblical correction from mentors focuses on your "do," not your "who." In other words, their correction focuses on what you did, not who you are. It focuses on your decision making and not your personal worth. In other words, why would you make such a low decision when you have such a high calling?

Remember, correction is not rejection, but protection and direction!

The Bible tells us in John 16:22, "And ye now therefore have sorrow: but I will see you again, and your heart shall rejoice, and your joy no man taketh from you." Throughout the years, I have been persecuted and lied about by many. I remember when I was first radically saved. I had been living completely sold out to the devil, so I figured I might as well be completely sold out to God! At the time, I would tell anything that moved about Jesus and my conversion. I still do; I just have a little bit more tact (see Colossians 4:5).

> *Correction is not rejection, but protection and direction!*

Since the age of 15, I have always been highly involved in weight training and body weight calisthenics, so some of my first "targets" for Jesus were bodybuilders at the gym to which I belonged. I remember talking to one of my weight lifting buddies about Jesus. He was very receptive. Just as I was making some progress toward leading him to Jesus, along came two other guys that I worked out with. Unfortunately, they were very drunk. They had heard of my conversion and saw me talking to our mutual friend about Jesus. They jumped out of their truck and began to mock me viciously. It was only a few months after I received Christ. Before I was born again, I would have fought both of them at the same time.

However, I knew that would not be a good witness for our Lord. This was the very first time I was persecuted for my new found faith. Up to that point, I had been fairly well received.

I remember driving in my car feeling every bit of joy I had in my soul running down my leg and out of my life. Thank God for Matthew 5:12–14: "Rejoice, and be exceeding glad: for great is your reward in heaven; for so persecuted they the prophets which were before you. Ye are the salt of the earth; but if the salt has lost his savor, wherewith shall it be salted? It is henceforth good for nothing, but to be cast out, and to be trodden under foot of men. Ye are the light of the world. A city that is set on a hill cannot be hid."

When you are persecuted for righteousness' sake (not for being a "Christian jerk" who doesn't know the difference between "telling it like it is" and *loving* boldness— see Ephesians 4:15), you must rejoice because great is your reward in heaven! Let no man steal your joy.

The Bible tells us, "To the praise of the glory of his grace, wherein he hath made us accepted in the beloved" (Ephesians 1:6). Remember, when you are accepted by the Best, who cares about the rest? Popularity is when you are liked by others. Security is when you are liked by yourself. Maturity is when you know you are loved by God.

If you are continually getting kicked in the rear, chances are you are out front *leading*! Never let people steal your joy.

CHAPTER

14

Sow It!

Sow where you want to go!

As a pastor, you can't always teach "cotton candy" messages. Many times, I have to give those "broccoli" messages. You know, the kind you don't want to swallow, but you know they are good for you. It's my assignment as a pastor to teach the "whole counsel of God" (see Acts 20:27), not just bits and pieces. There are times when I am ministering a "broccoli" message that I don't always get the positive reinforcement I am looking for! I fully understand what Jeremiah meant when he said, "Lord deliver me from their faces" (Jeremiah 1:8).

Over decades of ministry, I have truly seen some "faces." I've seen sleeping faces, I've seen angry faces, I've seen bored faces (and those are just from my wife)—I've even seen a guy lean back in his chair right in the middle of what I thought was a wonderful sermon and put two quarters on his eyes! I've seen people picking their noses as my gaze falls upon them in the middle of my anointed message.

From time to time, I will teach one of those messages where I feel like I am "plowing ground," and the highest accolade I will receive is a tepid "golf clap." After one of these messages, I will call my answering machine at my house and leave myself an encouraging message. I'll know I've left it, but I will still see the flashing light on my machine indicating I have a message waiting. Even though I left it, I still get pretty excited about the encouragement to come!

Before you think I'm the weird one, do you remember what the Bible says in 1 Samuel 30:6–8? "David encouraged himself in the Lord." David was going through one of the lowest points in his life, yet he knew the power of encouragement. Sometimes, you have to be your own cheerleader! Two, four, six, eight, who do I appreciate? Me!

You can't give what you don't have, and if you are not encouraged, you certainly won't be able to give it away!

> *Sometimes, you have to be your own cheerleader!*

I have a personal goal that when you are in my presence for at least one minute, I want to in some way encourage you! I don't do this perfectly, but I do this consistently. It may not be some pearl of wisdom that will forever change your life, but my desire is to at least leave you lifted.

I remember reading a powerful story about a book publisher who worked for two very famous ministers. This publisher published books for the first minister for ten years, and every time they got together, all this pastor ever talked about was himself or his ministry. The publisher said, "After ten years, he doesn't know me any more than the day I first walked into his office."

The second minister is extremely well known throughout the world. The publisher was recalling his initial meeting with this world-renowned minister. The publisher was quite nervous, but when this man of God walked in, he quickly introduced himself and then proceeded to ask the publisher (with genuine interest) all about this man's life. The publisher left encouraged. Today, the first pastor's ministry is almost non-existent, while the second minister is still touching the world for Jesus Christ!

There are two kinds of people in life:

1. Those who, when you leave their presence, leave you feeling better about *them*.

2. Those who, when you leave their presence, leave you feeling better about *you*!

The Bible says in Proverbs 12:25, "Heaviness in the heart of man maketh it stoop: but a good word maketh it glad." Here is what I've found about this powerful verse: not only does it make the heart of the one you are encouraging glad, but it will make your heart glad, too!

I discovered a long time ago that with one minor exception, the world's entire population consists of someone other than you. When you are always wrapped up with yourself, you make for one small package!

"You don't understand!" you might say. "I'm the one that needs joy." Great, give it away! When I was going through all of those very serious heart challenges that I discussed earlier, it was the most difficult time of my life. It would have been very easy to get discouraged and lose my joy. However, one thing I actually looked for during that dark time was other people who were struggling with cardiovascular disease. When I found them, I would always go out of my way to pray for *them*. The Bible tells us to pray one for another that *you* may be healed (see James 5:16). In other words, sow where you want to go!

> *With one minor exception, the world's entire population consists of someone other than you.*

There are many reasons people don't encourage others, but there are five primary reasons we must identify and overcome.

1. Personal insecurity.

Hurting people hurt people, but whole people help people. When you understand just how much you are loved by God, and when you understand who you are in Christ, it's easy to give encouragement to others.

2. Failure to value people properly.

The value of something is always determined by the price that was paid for it. Jesus paid the highest price for others: His life. That makes *people* God's most valuable possession!

3. Improper view of God.

If we think God is a car-wrecking, cancer-causing Creator and not a loving, life-giving Lord, then we are going to have a difficult time valuing people. We treat people how we think God treats us. Remember, God is not mad at you; He is madly in love with you!

4. Selfishness

Followers think mostly about themselves. Leaders think mostly about others.

5. "That's not my personality"

The Bible tells us, "Encourage one another daily while it is called today" (Hebrews 3:13). It does not say, "Encourage one another daily while it is called today... unless that's not your personality!" It may not come naturally to you, but you can choose to encourage.

Don't misunderstand me; I am not talking about flattery (see Proverbs 29:5). Flattery takes; encouragement gives. True biblical encouragement is so powerful!

- People want to do the right thing... stand with them.
- People want to achieve things they can be proud of... motivate them.
- People want to belong to a team that achieves the extraordinary... invite them.
- People want to make a difference for the Lord... inspire them!

Just like you, I have many opportunities to be discouraged and let go of my joy. However, one of my secrets for being so joyful is I don't think a whole lot about myself. I don't mean that I don't create some borders and margin in my personal life, and I don't mean that I don't need a little "me" time on occasion, but I do mean that self-centered people are the most miserable people I know!

When was the last time you were in a really lousy mood? As I said before, when we are in truly bad moods, we are thinking about ourselves!

I have hundreds of "Pastor Jim cards"—little cards that I keep in my office and at my house. Whenever I feel discouragement trying to crawl up my hind leg and joy trying to climb down it, I simply get out my "Pastor Jim cards" and begin writing encouraging notes to others. Not an email or a text, but a handwritten note. Normally, by about the second or third encouraging note, I can feel discouragement crawl back down to the devil where it belongs and joy sink back into my soul where it belongs!

If you truly need joy, give it away! If you are truly tired of *enduring* life and want to begin *enjoying* life,

- Define it!

- Recognize you already have it!

- Choose it!

- Speak it!

- Repeat it!

- Renew it!

- Praise it!

- Laugh at it!

- Don't leak it!

- Make it!

- Don't let people steal it!

- Sow it!

Then you, too, will never be down, discouraged, or depressed another day in your life!

Jim Frease and his wife Anne, and their son, Johnathan.

ABOUT THE AUTHOR

Jim Frease is the Founder and Senior Pastor of Joy Church in Mt. Juliet, Tennessee, and Founder and President of World Changers Bible Institute (WCBI).

He is also the founder of Joy Ministerial Exchange (JME), a ministerial organization designed to impart to pastors from across the country.

Jim emphasizes a relationship with Jesus Christ, not religion; the Word of God, not tradition; and he emphasizes enjoying one's life, not enduring it. He teaches not just what to do, but how.

Jim and his wife Anne have been married since 1990 and deeply love their son, Johnathan. Jim loves spending time with his family, and enjoys Ohio State football, fishing, Ohio State football, fishing, and Ohio State football. Anne loves to shop. Sometimes, they compromise and shop at Bass Pro.

Most importantly, Jim and Anne are deeply in love with the Lord Jesus Christ and are completely committed to His Word. As they minister, they do so with humor & joy (Nehemiah 8:10) and integrity (Psalm 26:11), propelling the listener to a greater intimacy with Jesus.

ABOUT JOY CHURCH

Based out of Mt. Juliet, Tennessee,
Joy Church is a rapidly growing, multi-generational,
multicultural church with people from almost every
denominational background—including those with
no church background at all.

At Joy Church, we don't believe in organized religion;
we believe in organized relationship with God the Father
through His Son, Jesus Christ.

We are not about tradition, but the liberating Word of God.
We are not about enduring life—we are about enjoying life!

For more information, please visit joychurch.net